PLAY SHOWTIME

Hits from the Greatest Shows of All Time

For Cello with Piano accompaniment
arranged by Pat Legg and Alan Gout

Contents

© 1998 by Faber Music Ltd
First published in 1998 by Faber Music Ltd
Bloomsbury House 74–77 Great Russell Street London WC1B 3DA
Music processed by Chris Hinkins
Printed in England by Caligraving Ltd
All rights reserved

ISBN10: 0-571-51851-6
EAN13: 978-0-571-51851-7

FABER **ff** MUSIC

The Lambeth Walk
(Me And My Girl)

Music and original lyrics
by Noel Gay

People Will Say We're In Love
(Oklahoma!)

Music by Richard Rodgers
Original lyrics by Oscar Hammerstein II

If I Were A Rich Man

(Fiddler On The Roof)

Music by Jerry Bock
Original lyrics by Sheldon Harnick

Tonight
(West Side Story)

Music by Leonard Bernstein
Original lyrics by Stephen Sondheim

Younger Than Springtime

(South Pacific)

Music by Richard Rodgers
Original lyrics by Oscar Hammerstein II

Memory
(Cats)

Music by Andrew Lloyd Webber
Original lyrics by Trevor Nunn, after T.S. Eliot

I Could Have Danced All Night

(My Fair Lady)

Music by Frederick Loewe
Original lyrics by Alan Jay Lerner

16

Waltz – Love Unspoken
(The Merry Widow)

Music by Franz Lehár
Original lyrics by Viktor Léon and Leo Stein

Don't Cry For Me Argentina
(Evita)

Music by Andrew Lloyd Webber
Original lyrics by Tim Rice

As Long As He Needs Me

(Oliver!)

Music and original lyrics
by Lionel Bart

UNBEATEN TRACKS

8 contemporary pieces for Cello and Piano

Edited by Steven Isserlis

ISBN 0-571-51976-8

Unbeaten Tracks for cello brings the diverse world of contemporary music within the reach of the less-experienced player (around Grades 4 to 7). The eight pieces in the volume – all specially commissioned by world-famous cellist Steven Isserlis – are written in an array of musical styles by some of today's most talented composers.

Steven Isserlis: 'I am delighted with this collection of weird and wonderful pieces – a collection that I hope will come to be viewed as staple repertoire for cello students, as well as fascinating encores for professionals (I'm already performing several of them regularly). One of the qualities that I find most appealing in this volume is the variety of musical personalities that shine through each offering …'

Carl Davis	*Elegy*
Lowell Liebermann	*Album leaf, Op.66*
Olli Mustonen	*Frogs dancing on water lilies*
John Woolrich	*Cantilena*
Julian Jacobson	*Hip hip bourrée*
Mark-Anthony Turnage	*Vocalise*
David Matthews	*Tango flageoletto*
Steven Isserlis	*The haunted house*